Adopting a Child with a Trauma and Attachment Disruption History:

A Practical Guide

Theresa Ann Fraser, C.Y.W, M.A., C.P.T.
A Biological, Foster, and Adoptive Parent

Foreword by William E. Krill, LPC

Adopting A Child With A Trauma And Attachment Disruption History: A Practical Guide
Copyright © Theresa Ann Fraser 2012. All Rights Reserved.
Foreword by William E. Krill, LPC

Learn more at www.TheresaFraser.com

ISBN-13: 978-1-61599-130-3 (trade paper)
eISBN: 978-1-61599-131-0 (ebook)

Published by
Loving Healing Press
5145 Pontiac Trail
Ann Arbor, MI 48105

www.LHPress.com
Tollfree 888-761-6268
Fax 734-663-6861

To request a free evaluation copy or purchase multiple copies for a non-profit or service agency at a special discount, please contact us through info@LHPress.com.

Distributed by Ingram Book Group (USA/CAN), Bertram's Books (UK), Hachette Livre (FR), Agapea (SP), Angus & Robertson (AU).

Distributed by Ingram Book Group (USA/CAN), Bertram's Books (UK

Contents

Foreword	iii
How Does Trauma Impact the Development of Attachment?	1
"Every Family is a Country"	2
What pre-training doesn't prepare you for	3
First Days: Rules, Structure and Routines= SAFETY	6
Simple Ways to build trust	8
First Months: Relationship Building	9
Involve your new child in the family narrative.	9
Creating your child's special space in the home.	9
Facilitating Attachment	10
Birth Families	10
Talking about Biological Family	11
Relationship Building with others	12
Lessons and Extracurricular Activities	13
When extra help is needed	13
Resources for the Adoptive Parent	15
Safety	15
Structure	15
Supervision	15
Support	16
Questions parents should ask and discuss prior to the new child joining the family.	17
In Closing	17
Appendix: Resiliency Checklist for Children	19
References	20
Web Resources	21
About the Author	22

Contents

Foreword iii
How Does Trauma Impact the Development of Attachment? 1
"Every Family is a Country" 2
What pre-training doesn't prepare you for 3

First Days: Rules, Structure and Routines = SAFETY 6
Simple Ways to build trust 8

First Months: Relationship Building 9
Involve your new child in the family narrative 9
Creating your child's special space in the home 9
Facilitating Attachment 10
Birth Families 10
Talking about Biological Family 11
Relationship Building with others 12
Lessons and Extracurricular Activities 13
When extra help is needed 13

Resources for the Adoptive Parent 15
Safety 15
Structure 15
Supervision 15
Support 16
Questions parents should ask and discuss prior
to bringing child/youth into family 17

In Closing 17
Appendix: Resiliency Checklist for Children 19
References 20
Web Resources 21
About the Author 23

Foreword

Adoptive and foster parents are the salt of the earth. I am convinced that people who take in children who are not their own are not *made*, they are *born*. There is a singular quality to foster and adoptive parents, and that is the ability to not only tolerate, but work at *healing* the many wounds that such children bring in through their doors. And while this takes an uncommon degree of compassion and skill, it all begins with love.

Fostering and adopting parents have love for more than just the child. Through taking in these children, they also express a love for their immediate communities and the world. The work they do is of incalculable value, both in terms of money and the community. Institutionalized care of these children would surely be a tax burden for the community beyond compare, and the human cost in society of damaged individuals who in all likelihood would perpetuate the burden and damage is unimaginable.

Support for adoptive and fostering families is often slim to none. Those who do have good support systems should thank their lucky stars. Respect from the larger system, if respect is measured by systemic support, is usually marginal. The systems of foster care and adoption vary from state to state. In some places, there are financial discouragements to adopting children instead of simply fostering them (though some are called only to foster and not adopt). Indeed, in some places, when it comes to the financial support of the foster caregiver, it is actually more financially lucrative to keep children emotionally unstable and in "therapeutic foster care" than it is to have them move (often in the same household) to regular foster care. Once adopted, the funds for the child's care are either drastically cut, or dry up entirely. Yet foster parents keep fostering and adoptive parents dive into adoption. The common denominator, of course, is not money but love.

Yet love is not enough. Perhaps in days gone by, just loving a child and providing this young person with the basics of life and structure were enough. But those days are gone. Most children who find themselves in foster care are not there because they have been literally orphaned. They are there because they have been orphaned in a different way: through neglect, physical or sexual abuse, or their families were simply so chaotic with the outcomes of mental illness or addiction that they were no longer safe in their family environment. Often, these damages started even before the child was born. Stressed pregnancies have their sources in all kinds of sad and frightening circumstances, from an addicted mother to one who is in an emotionally or physically abusive relationship. In many cases, this is the only life the child has ever known.

The entire process of foster care and adoption, while having the *potential* for joyous and positive outcome, can be an addition of insult to injury at the very least, and at its worse, a continuation of the interpersonal trauma that the original removal was meant to protect the child from. And trauma it is, often fitting the criteria of Acute Stress Disorder or Post Traumatic Stress Disorder. Indeed, most folks who have been in the work of fostering children will tell you that a third diagnosis should be added, perhaps termed "Rolling Stress Disorder," to help define the truth of what it is for these children to have lived chaotic lives with their parent(s) and then multiple moves from foster home to foster home, ever being disappointed in not finding a "forever home."

Giving care to such a child takes skill, and seasoned veterans of foster care will tell you that you can never have enough skill; the cases *are* getting more difficult year by year. In this small volume that Fraser is offering, there is a wondrous, compact "quick start" kit for both new and seasoned foster-adoptive parents. Theresa Fraser's straightforward and practical sensibilities flow from not only her academic credentials, but also from the compassion and experience of being a parent. This can be clearly read between the lines.

More than providing a behavioral-how-to-cookbook, Fraser has conveyed the more nuanced issues of pairing practical behavioral preparedness and positive, preventative interventions with the truth that the key between parent and child is attachment and authenticity in the developing relationship. Without the development of authenticity and emotional connection, foster care becomes the dreaded warehousing the media is fond of covering. She has described a treatment plan that balances high structure and high nurture; the need of which every foster parent intuitively knows, but cannot always articulate. If you have found this little book, you have found the way to articulate the plan so that you can carry it out...with your love as the foundational ingredient.

William E. Krill, LPC,
author *Gentling: A Practical Guide to Treating PTSD in Abused Children, 2nd Ed*

How Does Trauma Impact the Development of Attachment?

The work of the National Institute for Trauma and Loss and The Child Trauma Academy have increased our understanding of how early life experiences or lack of experiences impact the development and wiring of a child's brain. If a child is highly defensive and often in a state of freeze (Perry, Szalavitz, 2006), it makes sense that relationship building will be more challenging. It is difficult to relax and enjoy the moments and experiences around us if we feel that we are in a state of alarm or are at risk of being hurt.

Little people who have lived in a chronic situation of abuse or neglect don't understand what a caring relationship is like. They enter into the adoptive home expecting the worst: adults are to be feared and not trusted. If they meet one adult who differs from this well-reinforced self-protective template (such as a foster parent or a kind teacher) they may feel that this one individual is very different from the rest. This one positive experience does not transform the child's perceptions. Unfortunately it is going to take many positive experiences for this child's worldview to change and include new parents as people one can really depend on.

"Bonding involves a set of behaviours that will help lead to forming an attachment (Perry, N.D.) p. 2.". Dr. Perry goes on to describe attachment as being a:

- special form of an enduring relationship with a special person
- involves soothing, comfort and pleasure
- loss or threat of loss of this specific person evokes distress, the child finds security and safety in the context of this relationship.

Dr. Perry and others stress that if physical and emotional safety can be created, the power of relationship and love can change the traumatized child.

Parents also need to be cognizant that not all children react to a traumatic event in the same way.

> Henri (age 4) and his brother Luis (age 3) were apprehended from marijuana growing house. When born, Luis had both marijuana and Demerol in his system. Child Protection authorities found the children locked in a back room with feces and urine everywhere. There was water in a pitcher with a few cups, but no

food or evidence of food (dishes, packaging) to be seen. When the children entered foster care, their first family noted that both boys hid food in their room. Luis had bi-monthly trips to the hospital for an impacted bowel because he kept continuously eating, and still begged for food in whatever setting he was in.

The agency wanted to keep the children together. Their behaviours were viewed to be so extreme that they were not viewed as appropriate for adoptive placements. They were placed in a long-term treatment foster home at ages 5 and 7. Even years later, Louis would eat meals quickly unless adults reminded him to slow down. He experienced extreme anxiety symptoms when food was placed in front of him, such as when his foster family took him to Disney World and they attended family style restaurants.

Henri has no food issues, yet he grew up in the same family and shared the traumatic experience of his sibling. Why?

> With resilience, children can triumph over trauma; without it, trauma (adversity) triumphs. The crises children face both within their families and in their communities can overwhelm them (John, 1997)

Look to Appendix # 1 for resiliency factors.

"Every Family is a Country"

The analogy that every family is a country helps both parents and kids understand that adding a family member or joining a new family takes some adjustment, especially during the immigration phase (Fraser, 2010). As you might expect, each country has its own king, queen, sheriff, currency, language etc.

We forget that new family members have already visited a country prior to joining ours. A child with trauma and attachment disruption may have lived in many countries, and at times forgets what the language or currency is for the current one.

> Emily joined her adoptive family at five after living in a foster placement for two years. In her family of origin her father and teenage brother had sexually abused her. When she wanted something purchased for her, she would attempt to rub the genitals of her adoptive Dad even though this behavior had been extinguished in foster care. When upset, she also would masturbate much to the embarrassment of her adoptive mom. The masturbating decreased as her anxiety decreased and her comfort

level in the home increased. The inappropriate touching decreased as Dad was able to set firm limits and guidelines about how she could get things purchased for her. It took some time for Emily to believe that sexual favors were not the currency in this family.

What pre-training doesn't prepare you for

We need to be reminded that adopting a child who has had multiple caregivers (not necessarily attachment figures) is challenging. Often during first few days, weeks or months of a placement, new adoptive parents describe adding a child to their family as being a "smooth transition." Then the "honeymoon" is over, which means that previously documented behaviours may re-emerge or new ones may be observed.

New parents may then see the child as being manipulative, given they were able to follow rules during the honeymoon phase. However, this next phase (of challenging behaviour) is actually healthy, because this means that the child believes that their presence in this family is real. They are no longer visitors. Hence they will test out rules, roles and expectations in order to ascertain where they fit into this new family dynamic.

Children who have a history of trauma and attachment disruption are often skilled at recognizing what trigger or button will create the most impact. If manners are important in your family system, they might be challenged. If church attendance or respecting the Ten Commandments (by refraining from saying the Lord's name in vain) is a value, the child will rebel against them. Essentially, whatever holds meaning is up for challenge as the child attempts to ascertain where his meaning fits in the family's values and beliefs.

> Shane was twelve years old when he joined his new family as an only child. His adoptive Dad was a Chef but Shane announced that he had now become a vegetarian and was not interested in most of the meals that were prepared for him. His parents decided not to engage in power struggles with him and just explained the nutritional pyramid so Shane could choose protein items that were not meat. In time, because it was not an issue, Shane began to sample some of his new Dad's meals.

Food and expulsion are two areas where kids can have control. The new and wise parent will set some guidelines but ensure that the child feels that they have some power somewhere in the eating and toileting domains.

Fifteen-year-old Sam knew that family meals were a priority for his new adoptive family where he was the only son with three adolescent siblings and two working parents. Just prior to signing adoption papers, he began to skip dinners and later would complain that he didn't have time to talk for thirty minutes hence he could get his nutritional needs met by eating left-overs when they returned from seeing friends or volunteering. He also began to be late for curfew but would always return just before a Missing Person's police report needed to be filed.

Sam ended up requesting to be returned to foster care, but later went back to the adoptive home after he agreed to sign a contract that outlined familial expectations. He told his therapist that he thought the returning process was odd, since he'd chosen to leave and thought it should be his independent decision as to whether he returned to his adoptive family. He didn't understand that unmet emotional needs of other family members also had to be considered in the family dynamic.

New parents should be encouraged to enjoy the honeymoon phase. This time period lays a positive foundation for creating a family identity, identifying commonalities and common interests and essentially beginning to determine the things that you love about each other. Developing these areas are important, given conflict usually arises once the child has moved on from the honeymoon phase. If there is little foundation laid for relationship building, the emerging behaviors become more challenging for new parents.

An emergency consultation was requested when six year old Frankie had held scissors up to the throat of a classmate only a week after being placed in his adoptive home with his two older brothers.

After a classroom observation, it was clear that Frankie needed his routines simplified. In his new Grade One class, he had one teacher for the morning and a different teacher in the afternoon. His adoptive mom identified that during the first week of placement (which occurred on a school break) he'd always appeared tired and grouchy in the afternoon. The boy whom he had threatened to hurt was also quite busy if not annoying and bossy toward Frankie. It was therefore recommended that Frankie be moved to a table of quieter girls whom he would less likely be in conflict with at school. Additionally, it made sense to have him go home after the morning time period. This afforded him lunch daily with his new mom as well as a one to one afternoon with her. Within a few weeks his attitude at school was reported to have greatly improved and many afternoons he had a nap. His adoptive mom shared that this one to one time also gave her and Frankie a chance to be closer. Therefore, thinking outside of the box helped the school community to see Frankie more positively. Frankie and his mother also participated in six sessions of Theraplay©. During the last two months of school, he was slowly integrated into an afternoon schedule as well and was reported to no longer be academically behind when he entered Grade Two.

First Days: Rules, Structure and Routines= SAFETY

Immediately a child placed in your home is the time to be clear about family and individual rules and expectations. Consistent routines and predictable structure in the home milieu contribute to creating a foundation of relational safety for your new child or children.

This means that the new parents need to figure out the developmentally appropriate bedtimes for their children. Previous caregivers of your child may also be able to assist you in determining the best bedtime, as some children need more or less sleep than their age peers.

Also, new adoptive parents often experience much of what biological parents of newborns do. Messing with the sleeping schedule by having too exciting a day impacts the child's ability to get to sleep or stay asleep. Often as a therapist, I invite the parents to learn about the steps involved in infant parenting and then to adapt these as required for the new older child.

> Sarah came to her first Parent Consultation in tears. She had read all the books she could on therapeutic and attachment based parenting. She was cautious about her voice tone and body language. However, her new nine-year-old son was not only NOT settling at night, but also demanding two hours of both her and her husband's time when they were exhausted. If Mom and Dad did not cooperate, James would have intense tantrums and was beginning to destroy his newly decorated room. The new parents were not getting any couple time, their sex life had deteriorated and though they were not arguing, they were not communicating much either.

I told Sarah, "If you don't structure James, he will structure you."

In other words, children who have experienced neglect or abuse often attempt to control many of the situations around them. This need to control is ultimately counterproductive because it can replicate their previous life experiences with parental figures, who had not been able to parent developmentally. These children benefit from knowing that their new parents know what is best and will ensure that what is best occurs.

Sarah needed assistance turning this negative pattern. Instead of lying with her son beside him on the bed and reading to him, the therapist suggested that a chair or rocking chair be added to his room. The parent could rock the child for a while or sit on the chair with feet on James' bed. Sarah was also instructed to have a book or writing available after story time so James got the message, "I am hear with you, I love you but I need to do some of my work now." Sarah reported that this routine improved James' ability to settle independently. Time spent in the room decreased from two hours to one and ultimately fifteen minutes. This gave Mom and Dad the opportunity to end the day with time spent supporting each other.

It is also important during the early days of relationship building that simple routines are established. As with newborn parents, adoptive parents want to introduce their child to their friends, family and significant others. It is also important to take things slowly with your adoptive child. Overwhelming the child will create anxiety that will manifest in behaviour that emerges the next day or a few days later.

New adoptive parents are also astonished at how easily their new children meet new people. In fact they may be asking to go home with them! This is very common for children who have had multiple caregivers. It almost appears as if the child is keeping their options open in case this family experience breaks down. So, keep expectations clear and don't personalize this survival behaviour. It is really not about you.

> Olivia reported that their seven-year-old daughter would leave her new parents at any group gathering and attempt to sit on the knee of other mothers or in between couples. Encouraging her to come back was met with dirty looks and pouting, not made easier by adults who reassures her parents that the girl was all right where she was.
>
> This therapist affirmed to Olivia that this habit would continue without intervention to change it. It is important that the adoptive parents let go of their own embarrassment or worry about being perceived as mean. They need to tell other adults that their kindness is appreciated but that they would like to spend time with their daughter.
>
> Shaun and Mary also reported that when they went anywhere (such as swimming at the lake) their nine-year-old son joined other families and ignored them. They felt rejected and waited for him to return. This happened when he needed something. Also, the boy had no problem asking the new family for drinks or meals.

It is therefore important for the new parents to talk about what will be happening at the activity ahead of time. It is also important to firmly lay out the expectations such as, "you will stay with your family and if you wander away we will call you back so we know you are safe. It is a parent's job to keep their kids safe."

Simple Ways to build trust

Children with multiple experiences of loss and rejection are unable to trust that their new "parents" will keep them safe and provide them with loving care. They are often hypervigilent and not open to letting parents zip zippers or button buttons. They often will not ask for support regarding unmet needs.

New parents often take this personally, rather than recognizing that the child's worldview needs to grow, and will do so in time. This growth can be facilitated when parents quietly anticipate their child's needs while also following through on meeting these. For example, if you have promised to pick up a binder, or to watch a soccer game, do your best to follow through. Your child undoubtedly expects you not to. Therefore, provide many repetitive experiences that communicate, *I am here for you and will take care of you.* This will assist your child in changing this world view. Trust takes time. An old adage that fits here is "fake it until you make it." Respond to your child as if you were trustworthy, but also as if he trusted you, and this will become stronger. Your child is watching you when you don't think he is.

First Months: Relationship Building

Involve your new child in the family narrative.

An adoptive child may have joined the family story in Chapter five and doesn't know what has come before. Often new adoptive parents create a family scrapbook explaining how they'd first met, when they decided to adopt or how they felt the very first time they heard about their new child. You don't need to create a scrapbook, but remember to share with your child these very important stories that biological children may have already heard multiple times.

It is also helpful to have pictures of key members of the extended family, so that the child has some advance information about who these folks are when she attends a larger family gathering. Sometimes having a little blurb of information to go along with the photo can be quite helpful and will also decrease the child's anxiety when she attends a gathering where these folks will be present.

Creating your child's special space in the home.

After your child has settled in may be a good time to redecorate the child's room, involving him to participate in the process. Everything is very new and can be overwhelming in the beginning, hence not as appreciated by the new child. By waiting, you are truly involving your child because during the early days he may just make choices he thinks that you like.

That said, suppose you have a child who always asks for the third unoffered choice after you have offered two. This may be the child you decorate the room for.

Ask for a paint color he likes and go from there, not expecting too much appreciation. Children who have experiences of neglect may present as being quite entitled, which is often a counter-reaction to their deprived environmental histories. This can be confusing for new parents who feel like they have provided their new children with opportunities or things they may never have had before.

New parents are cautioned as well not to go "overboard" spending lots on furniture and furnishing, particularly if your new child is known to destroy items during tantrums.

Facilitating Attachment

Comparing adoption with arranged marriages often helps parents understand why they don't have an instant emotional connection with their chosen child.

If we just took the mom from one family and placed her in another, there is no guarantee that the husband and wife would like each other let alone love each other. The rules and routines might not make sense.

It is the same with adoption. Trying to work on liking each other is more important than loving each other. Loving takes time.

Play is a great place to begin when there is frustration and resentment between family members. Quiet play is even better as a beginning. That way your child cannot set up power struggles or arguments. Therefore chess, checkers, walking or anything other activity that doesn't require verbal interaction is recommended at least a few times a week. If your child begins to engage verbally with you, follow her lead.

Birth Families

If the child has not pulled out photos of birth family members, this may be a good time to do so. If, however, don't do this if previous therapists or other adults involved with the child has advised against it.

> Devante had lived in multiple foster homes and his last foster home was against adoption and predicted that it wouldn't last. The adoptive parents felt quite intimidated by these previous caregivers, but also recognized the strong commitment they had made to this child's happiness. If they could have adopted, this family would have liked to adopt Devante but not his older brother, hence an adoptive home was sought for both children. When the boys were placed together, a photo of them with the foster parents was placed in a nice frame and hung in their room. Over time Devante took the picture down, saying that he felt sad looking at it even though he was happy in his new home.

These ambivalent feelings are common for adoptive children. To have loved many previous caregivers and to have lost them can at times prevent children from emotionally investing in their adoptive relationships. If current caregivers can reassure the child that he doesn't have to choose, especially if others have said they do, in time they will trust the inner feelings of safety that are being established.

> Eight-year-old Andrea was told by her birth mother at their good bye visit that she never had to share her heart with another

mother. When she was eighteen, they would find each other again. This parting message took Andrea a long time to let go of. She needed adoptive parents who could accept this and also give her the message that she could add loving caregivers in her life without replacing old ones.

Robert was using the family computer one day and found the open Facebook™ account of his 12-year-old adoptive son Evan. Evan had many friends including his biological grandmother who he had recently and quietly found. Robert, though hurt, negotiated with grandmother that contact could be maintained provided that Robert was also listed as a "friend" on both grandmother and son's account. Though many may disagree with this approach, it provided Robert with the opportunity to supervise this initial underground relationship while also giving Evan the message that he was not threatened by contact but wanted it to be positive for Evan.

Facebook™ is a powerful people connector, and more and more individuals in the adoption triangle (biological parent, adoptive parent, adoptee) are finding each other. All parents need to establish rules in their household while providing their children with good supervision. Ensuring that your kids are only connecting with those they are supposed to is of great importance, because once they know "how to open the gate, they have left the farm." It is hard to pull them back, so talk with members of your adoption team (therapist, child welfare worker, child's teacher) and find out what they think is in your child's best interest based on his safety and security.

"Although online social networking is all the rage, real world friendships and relationships apparently aren't doing so well." (Perry, Szalavitz, 2010, p3). Therefore, providing limits around online interacting, and balancing this with time spent online with real time interactions makes sense for the child who is struggling with relationship development.

Talking about Biological Family

As your child grows, he will gain more understanding about what adoption means. Being honest about your child's story while respecting the biological family can be a challenge, given we don't want our adopted children fantasizing about the parent they will find (if they choose to) when they reach 18. Therefore, having an idea of what you can say when the time comes is important. For example, "your mother has had five children taken from her because she isn't able to take care of them or keep them safe. I wonder sometimes if this is because no one ever taught her how." This gives an honest message but also a context. If children aren't provided a context, they will invent their own.

Holidays provide an opportunity to remind children that you are able to honor the people who made them. For example, on birthdays or Mother's Day, adoptive parents can give thanks or toast birth parents.

Compliments can also be given saying things like, "You have beautiful eyes, I wonder if your birth mother or father gave you those?" Or, "Your musical talents must have come from someone in your heritage."

Relationship Building with others

It is truly important for you and your child to develop connections with teachers, coaches and tutors. Essentially, anyone your child is involved with needs to meet you, and although you do not need to share your child's history, it is important for others to know that you are an adoptive family.

> Amanda was six years old and attending her first summer day camp. When her adoptive mother arrived at camp to pick her up, the camp staff were quite secretive about where she was and then admitted that social services had picked her up.
>
> Patricia returned home and called their adoptive worker from Amanda's city of origin, who in turn contacted investigators from the local child protection agency. They had received a call from camp staff who had heard Amanda say that she'd seen her Dad murder her little brother. No one had asked Amanda which Dad. It never had crossed anyone's mind observing the strong connection between Mom and Dad and daughter that Amanda was adopted and therefore referring to her biological father.

Adoptive and foster children can also struggle at school during classes where family trees are constructed. It is therefore important to ask the school, perhaps during registration, where familial history fits into the curriculum. In some schools it is part of social studies and other schools religious studies. If adoptive parents know when this is coming up they can prepare the teacher as well as their child. It is therefore, also important for adoptive parents to inquire where biological family members grew up or currently reside so potential connections can be prepared for. The Centre for Adoption support and Education (C.A.S.E.)

provides a course for facilitators known as W.I.S.E. U.P. which assists parents and children in practicing strategies on how to respond to others about being adopted.

If your adopted child has a cultural or spiritual heritage different from your own, try to learn about it or connect with others who can educate the whole family. This information is not only enriching, but also says to the child that the parents love everything about her and want to share in this as she shares in their heritage.

Efforts like these can dispel anxiety, and counter previous messages that the child may have received about adoptive families making you forget where you have come from.

Lessons and Extracurricular Activities

If your child has a special talent or interest, by all means register him in a few activities. However, be cautious about over-programming your new child. One activity for personal development is appropriate during the first few months, especially if you have to return to work and your child will be registered in after school or daycare. These opportunities are already providing your child with interactional time with peers and other authority figures.

Your family time needs to be protected, but it can be loosely structured. Family game nights, walking around your neighborhood or biking instills good values about daily exercise. A family YMCA membership can be valuable but don't forget that time just relaxing together helps with relationship building.

When extra help is needed

Many families recognize after the honeymoon is over that it may be helpful to seek specific intervention. This can take many forms.

I have developed a model of service based on the following areas. Reviewing them helps to ascertain what the primary and/or secondary areas or perhaps multiple areas of concern are.

- the current and emerging parent/child relationship (with each parent in the family)
- the couple relationship
- adopted family identity in relation to child's biological family and/or most recent family (perhaps foster family)
- adopted family identity in relation to its extended families
- the new family's overall emerging identity

- the new or changed parent identity
- the child's or children's individual treatment Issues.

Once it is ascertained what area needs initial attention, the adoptive family can look for a Play Therapist who works with children and families, or an adoptive competent therapist who can help to focus on couple or individual parent issues. Whoever the clinician is, make sure you are comfortable with this person and choose someone who understands the complexity of adoption and adoptive families.

Resources for the Adoptive Parent
The Four S's: Safety, structure, supervision and support

Safety

Parenting children who have experienced trauma and/or attachment disruptions is not an easy journey. These children's survival behaviours can include stealing, lying, aggression, hoarding, as well as practicing a need to control what everyone around them is doing. They do not trust any adult to take care of them or anticipate their unmet needs.

This is the overwhelming task of the adoptive parent: to help this new child put his faith in them as parents who can protect, nurture and keep him safe. This task is difficult, and requires repetitive behavior from the new parent given their child lacks of experience with fair, predictable and nurturing caregivers.

These children see evidence of fairness and expect that something will be expected in return or that meanness will surface again soon. They then will expect that the behaviour won't last, and test the parent's ability to persevere with aforementioned responses. This is the time for new parents to be able to take a break, call on supports and attempt to balance their new responsibilities with individual, couple and family self-care.

Structure

Remember this phrase: "If you don't structure him, he will structure you?"

Children with trauma experiences need to know what is going on now and what is going to happen next. Predictability is reassuring, so both parents need to determine what the developmentally appropriate expectations are for their child and create routines around these decisions.

Supervision

Your child probably has visited many other kingdoms before yours. Often we assume that children will respond to the situations that confront them, the way we think that they will. Keep this in mind when attending family or group outings where other parents send their kids off to the basement to play. Your child may need modeling and boundaries in order to play in an age-appropriate manner. Your child may not even know how to play. This usually comes in time, but it is important to remember that structuring your home will help your child feel safe. When they are safe they will begin to risk trying new behaviours and some of these may not be healthy. Be there to provide your child with a healthy model and to provide a corrective experience.

It also is helpful when your child has consistency of caregivers.

Support

> Sam met with the Family Therapist alone, stating that being a new Dad was not what he expected it to be. Every morning began with tantrumming that lasted fifteen to forty-five minutes. His new son was aggressive towards his wife unless he was home, which made him late for work. His son was not affectionate and looked for every opportunity to argue or disagree with his new parents. He was really hoping that his new son would want to have a relationship with him and he felt that the boy gave every indication that he didn't want a relationship with them as evidenced by his behaviors.

The therapist pointed out to Sam that it is important for parents to fill their own cup up so to speak. Sam admitted that both he and his wife had stopped going on dates, their sex life had decreased and neither parent was participating in any of the individual activities they used to have prior to the adoption. These activities are all-important so that both Mom and Dad feel that they are getting some of their emotional needs met. This new relationship will take time for everyone to feel connected and begin to enjoy each other's company. It is therefore important for parents to not wait for this to happen by placing all their expectations on the new parent-child relationship. Make sure that each parent has independent time to visit friends and continue with hobbies as well as all-important couple time.

In order to accomplish this, the new family needs to have family members, friends or a good babysitter who can help out. Dealing with difficult behavior with no breaks is not good self-care.

It is also often helpful if adoptive families can connect with other adoptive families, either formally or informally. Common issues will be identified and peer support can help new parents feel less isolated and ineffectual.

New adoptive parents will also find some of the recent research on brain development in the face of neglect and abuse quite interesting and helpful. Google Dr. Bruce Perry or go to www.childtraumaacademy.org for online courses that can be taken at your own pace.

Questions parents should ask and discuss prior to the new child joining the family.

1. What are our expectations in regard to rules, routines and structure?
2. What are my important values I would want my child to share?
3. How do I expect to teach or share these with a child?
4. What rules, routines and structure are non-negotiable?
5. Who and what are our support systems?
6. Do I/we need to develop some additional support systems?
7. How are we going to ensure that we each have time to work on individual hobbies and interests?
8. Am I supportive of my partner's needs for self-care?
9. How are we going to ensure that we have couple time?
10. How do I feel about having contact with biological family members of an adopted child?
11. How is adoption going to change our family life, our marriage, our individual goals?
12. Am I personally, or we as a couple prepared to be emotionally rejected by a child?
13. When I think of a happy family, what does that look like?

It is helpful to journal the answers to these questions and then have a frank discussion with your partner. Discrepancies indicate that there needs to be further discussion, so agreement is achieved on how your family can operate with opposing opinions. It is healthy for parents to disagree and have a plan on how they can disagree respectfully.

In Closing

Being a parent is stressful. Parenting a child who has had a history of previous abuse or trauma can be extremely stressful, because this child requires much time prior to believing that these new parents can be trusted, and the child can expect to grow up with.

It is my experience that it often takes these special children at least two years before their mind and body identifies that this is the place where they will now live.

In these two years, the child will challenge and test out the parent-child relationship. Your child will require repetition, repetition, and more repetition in order to learn new skills and respond to their parents' attempts to keep him safe. Time does make the relationship stronger, and with time the confidence of both parents in their parenting role increases. Time also provides the opportunity for the child to feel more secure in her position in this family.

Your family's identity will also develop and solidify over this time.

Don't be shy, ask for ideas, resources and supports from other adoptive parents. Surf the web to find online resources. They are out there. Last but not least—Congratulations!

Appendix: Resiliency Checklist for Children

The following items were used in the International Resilience Project as a checklist for perceptions of resilience in children (Grotberg.E.) (N.D.) Often, children who have experienced attachment disruptions and traumatic experiences need additional experiences to develop these resiliency checklist items.

Checklist for Children

- The child has someone who loves him/her totally (unconditionally)
- The child has an older person outside the home she/he can tell about problems and feelings
- The child is praised for doing things on his/her own
- The child can count on her/his family being there when needed
- The child knows someone he/she wants to be like
- The child believes things will turn out all right
- The child does endearing things that make people like her/him
- The child believes in a power greater than seen
- The child is willing to try new things
- The child likes to achieve in what he/she does
- The child feels that what she/he does makes a difference in how things come out
- The child likes himself/herself
- The child can focus on a task and stay with it
- The child has a sense of humor
- The child makes plans to do things.

References

Fraser, T (2010) Every family is a country, in Lowenstein (Eds). *Creative Family and Therapy Techniques: Play, art and expressive activities to engage children in family sessions*, Champion Press. Toronto, Ontario.

Grotberg, E.H. (N.D.). *A guide to promoting resilience in children: strengthening the human spirit from Early Childhood development: practice and reflections,* Bernard Van Leer Foundation. The Hague: Netherlands
Retrieved August 10, 2011 from:
http://resilnet.uiuc.edu/library/grotb95b.html

John, M. (1997). A charge against society: The child's right to protection. London [u.a.: Kingsley.

Perry, B.D. (N.D.) Bonding and Attachment in Maltreated Children Consequences of Emotional Neglect in Childhood. Child Trauma Academy. Adapted in part from: *Maltreated Children: Experience, Brain Development and the Next Generation,* W.W. Norton & Company, New York, in preparation Retrieved August 17, 2011 from:
http://www.childtrauma.org/images/stories/Articles/attcar4_03_v2_r.pdf

Perry, B, D., Szalavitz,M. (2006) *The boy who was raised as a dog. And Other Stories from a Child Psychiatrist's Notebook: What Traumatized Children Can Teach Us About Loss, Love and Healing,* Basic Books. New York: N.Y.

Perry, B.C., Szalazitz, M. (2011) *Born for Love: Why Empathy Is Essential—and Endangered,* Harper Collins Publishers, New York: N.Y.

Web Resources

- Attachment Association of Canada
    http://www.attachmentcan.ca/
- Association for Child and Play Therapy:
    www.apt.org
- Attachment disorder information and support
    www.Attach.com
- Centre for adoption support and education
    www.adoptionsupport.org
- Canadian Association for Child and Play Therapy
    www.cacpt.com
- Changing Steps Counselling, Training and Consulting
    www.changing-steps.com
- Child Trauma Academy: This web site has up to date articles and courses for Professionals and parents regarding attachment and trauma.
    www.childtraumaacademy.org
- National Institute for Trauma and Loss
    www.starrtraining.org/tlc
- The Theraplay Institute
    www.theraplay.org

About the Author

Theresa graduated from Humber College in 1983 as a Child and Youth Worker. She has a B.A., Masters of Counselling Degree in Counselling Psychology and is a Canadian certified Child Psychotherapist and Play Therapist. In 2008, she was named the Clinical Specialist of the Year by the National Institute for Trauma and Loss. . She is the owner/lead therapist of her own agency www.changing-steps.com and a Professor at Sheridan College in Ontario, Canada. She wrote the bibliotherapy book, *Billy Had To Move* to help Child and Youth Workers, foster parents, social workers, and Play Therapists help children understand that they are not alone in their experiences or feelings.

Visit her site **www.theresafraser.com**

"I feel this book is great not only for children who are going through the loss of a loved one and having only strangers to turn to but also for children who have loving homes so they can better understand other children they may know who do live in foster care."
Virginia S. Grenier, *Stories For Children*

Available in paperback, hardcover and eBook editions
ISBN 978-1-932690-87-3
from Loving Healing Press
www.LHPress.com

Lightning Source UK Ltd.
Milton Keynes UK
UKOW06f0901150813

215230UK00009B/7/P